Save Our Animals!

Florida Manatee

Louise and Richard Spilsbury

Heinemann Library
Chicago, Illinois

Customer Service 888–454–2279

Visit our website at www.heinemannlibrary.com

Photo research by Hannah Taylor and Fiona Orbell
Designed by Michelle Lisseter and Ron Kamen
Printed in China, by South China Printing Co. Ltd.

10 09 08 07 06
10 9 8 7 6 5 4 3 2 1

Library of Congress Cataloging-in-Publication Data
Spilsbury, Louise.
Save the Florida manatee / Louise and Richard Spilsbury.
p. cm. -- (Save our animals!)
Includes bibliographical references and index.
ISBN-10: 1-4034-7806-6 (library binding-hardcover) ISBN-10: 1-4034-7814-7 (pbk.)
1. West Indian manatee--Juvenile literature. 2. West Indian manatee--Conservation--Juvenile literature. I. Spilsbury, Richard, 1963- II. Title. III. Series.

QL737.S63S65 2006
599.55--dc22

2005027998

Acknowledgments
The author and publisher are grateful to the following for permission to reproduce copyright material: Ardea pp. **4** top (Y A Betrand), **5** top left (J Rajput); Corbis pp. **6** (B D Cole), **27** (MacDuff Everton); Digital Vision p. **5** middle; Empics/AP Photo pp. **17** (P Cosgrove), **24** (SeaWorld Orlando); Florida Fish & Wildlife Conservation Commission p. **22**; FLPA/Minden Pictures pp. **11, 15** (F Bavendam); Naturepl.com pp. **4** bottom left (M Carwardine), **9, 12** (D Perrine), **14** (P Scoones), **16, 18** (J Foot); Nick Nottestad p. **26**; Oxford Scientific pp. **4** middle, **5** top right, **7, 13** (G Soury), **23, 25**; Photolibrary.com pp. **21, 28**; Still Pictures pp. **5** bottom, **10** (Dr. H Barnett), **19** (A & F Michler), **29** (D Faulkner).

Cover photograph of Florida manatee reproduced with permission of Corbis/Kennan Ward.

The publishers would like to thank staff at Save the Manatee for their assistance in the preparation of this book.

Some words are shown in bold, **like this**. You can find out what they mean by looking in the glossary.

Contents

Animals in Trouble

There are many different types, or **species**, of animals. Some species are in danger of becoming **extinct**. This means that all the animals from that species might die.

All the animals shown here are in danger of becoming extinct. These species need to be saved. The Florida manatee is one of them.

The Florida Manatee

Manatees are sometimes called sea cows. They live underwater and are as big as a small cow. They have wrinkly, gray skin and small eyes.

A Florida manatee has a large, flat mouth with whiskers around it.

Florida manatees move their tail up and down to swim.

The Florida manatee is one of four types of sea cows. Sea cows all look similar, but they live in different parts of the world.

Where Can You Find Florida Manatees?

Most Florida manatees live in or around the state of Florida. They live in areas of shallow, warm water, along **coasts**, and in rivers.

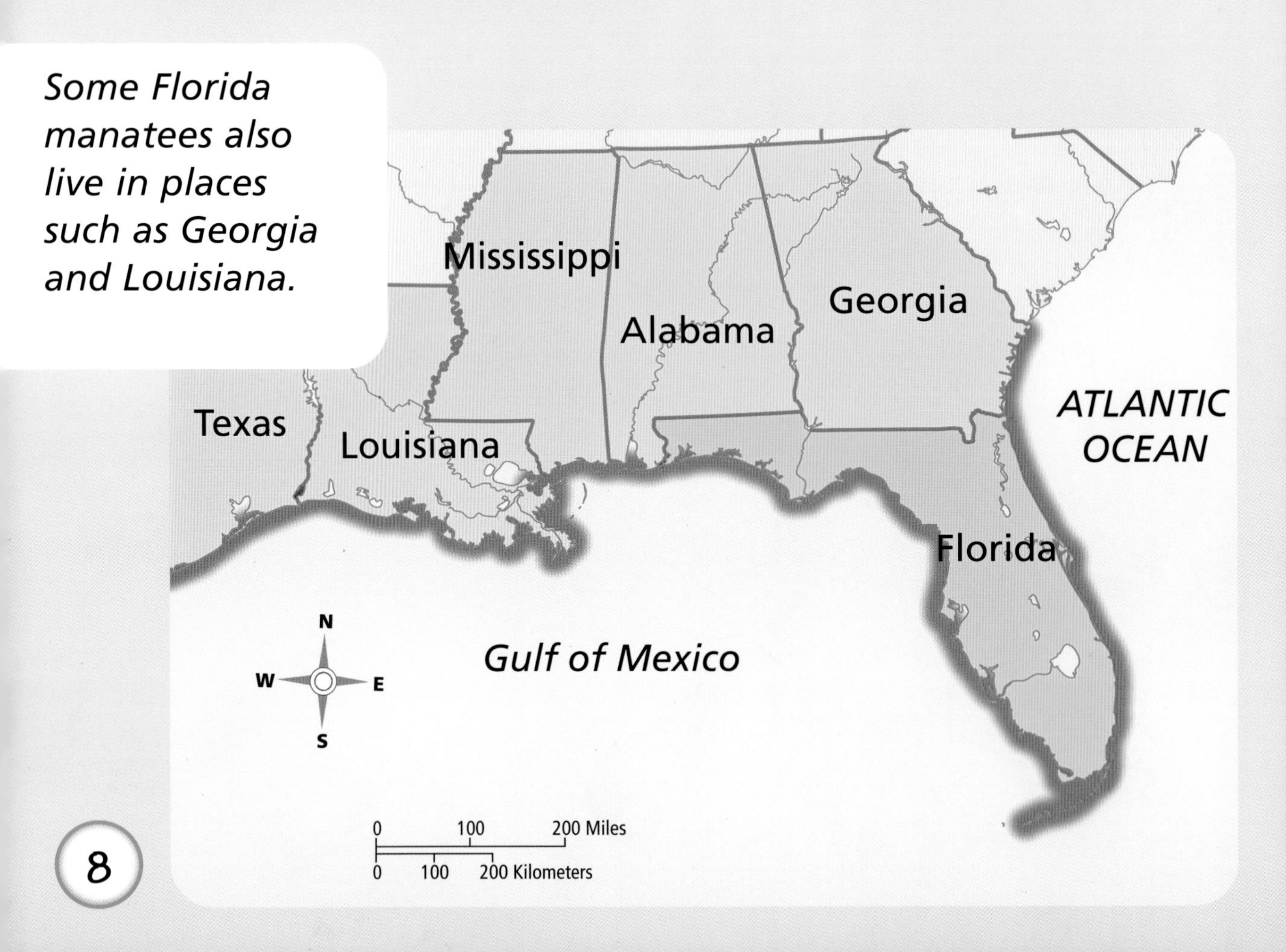

Some Florida manatees also live in places such as Georgia and Louisiana.

These Florida manatees have moved to warm water for the winter.

In summer many Florida manatees live in the ocean. In winter they **migrate** inland to warmer water in the rivers because the ocean gets too cold.

What Do Florida Manatees Eat?

Florida manatees are **herbivores,** which means they only eat plants. They eat huge amounts of sea grass and other water plants.

Manatees slowly push themselves along with their flippers as they feed.

Florida manatees eat for many hours every day. They hold plants with their two **flippers** and pull the leaves off using their lips. They chew with their big, flat teeth.

Florida manatees hold food with three nails at the end of each flipper.

Young Florida Manatees

Florida manatees are **mammals**, which means the babies feed on their mother's milk. A baby manatee is called a **calf**.

A manatee calf is born under the water. It comes to the surface to breathe air.

The mother manatee teaches her baby how to live safely.

A calf stays with its mother for two years. The mother teaches it which plants are safe to eat. She shows the calf where to find warm water in winter.

Natural Dangers

Young manatees can die if they do not learn where to find warm water and food. They are also in danger from wild animals that attack them.

Alligators will eat a baby manatee if they catch one.

Adult manatees are too big for alligators to attack. Adult manatees die if they get old or sick. Some manatees get sick if the water suddenly gets cold.

Adult manatees do not get attacked because they are so big.

Dangers from Water Sports

Sometimes speedboat drivers kill Florida manatees by accident. Their boats hit the manatees when they come to the surface to breathe.

Boat propellers can injure a manatee's soft skin.

This veterinarian is taking a fishing net off a Florida manatee.

Sometimes manatees get tangled in broken lines and old nets left by fishermen. These manatees die if they cannot eat or get to the surface for air.

Dangers to the Florida Manatee's World

Many people cut down the plants next to the **coast** or rivers, and build houses there. This leaves less food for the manatees to eat.

When people build on land near water, manatees cannot live there.

People can spoil water by putting garbage into it.

Some people dump waste in rivers and the ocean. This is called **pollution**. It can kill the water plants that manatees eat. It also makes manatees sick.

How Many Florida Manatees Are There?

In 1945 there were around 10,000 Florida manatees. Today there are just over 3,000.

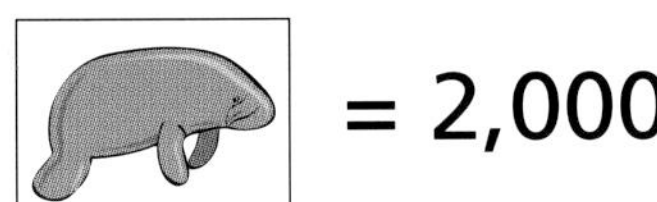

This graph shows how many Florida manatees are left.

When people saw that manatees were in danger, they began to help them. The number of manatees is growing very slowly.

Female *manatees only have one* ***calf*** *every few years.*

How Are Florida Manatees Being Saved?

Florida has laws to protect manatees. There are laws to stop people from dumping old fishing lines and hooks in the water, and to help stop **pollution** in the water.

This man is telling people in Florida how they can help protect manatees.

This sign tells boat drivers to slow down for manatees.

Some parts of Florida are watery **reserves** where boats are not allowed. Manatees can live safely there. In other areas, boats have to drive very slowly.

Who Is Helping Florida Manatees?

People in some wildlife parks help injured or sick Florida manatees. They care for them until they are well, then they set the manatees free.

People are putting this manatee back into the ocean now that it is better.

Save the Manatee is a **charity** that tells people about manatees and why they need help. It protects manatees and the places where they live.

*Charities work with **scientists** to find out more about Florida manatees.*

How Can You Help?

It is important to know that Florida manatees are in danger. Then you can learn how to help save them. Read, watch, and find out all you can about Florida manatees.

This class is doing a project on manatees.

Here are some things you can do to help.

- Join a **charity**, such as Save the Manatee. Can you raise money to save manatees?
- Visit wildlife parks or **reserves** where Florida manatees live safely. In some places you can even pay to swim with the manatees.

The Future for Florida Manatees

We must stop **pollution** in the ocean and rivers, and make sure we drive fast boats with care. If we do not, manatees may become **extinct**.

If there are too many people in Florida, will there be room for manatees?

Many people are working hard to save manatees. They hope that the number of Florida manatees will begin to grow if they are protected.

Let's hope that people will still be able to see these animals in the future.

Florida Manatee Facts

- Manatees are related to elephants. Their bones are like an elephant's, they have little hair, and their top lip moves a bit like a mini-trunk.
- Manatees can live for more than 60 years.
- A big manatee eats a lot of plants. It eats the same amount as 200 lettuces every day.
- Manatees can hold their breath underwater for several minutes before they need to come up for air.

Find Out More

Martin-James, Kathleen. *Gentle Manatees*. Minneapolis: Lerner, 2005.

Lithgow, John. *I'm a Manatee*. New York: Simon & Schuster, 2004.

Web Sites

To find out more about Save the Manatee, visit their Web site:

www.savethemanatee.org

Glossary

calf baby manatee

charity group that collects money and gives help to animals or people in need

coast area of land where it meets the ocean. Beaches are found along a coast.

extinct when all the animals in a species die out and the species no longer exists

female animal that can become a mother when it grows up. Women and girls are female people.

flippers front arms of a manatee

herbivore animal that only eats plants

mammal animal that feeds its babies on the mother's milk and has some hair on its body

migrate move to a different place to live for part of the year

pollution when something makes the land, rivers, oceans, or air dirty

reserve area where animals are protected

scientist person who studies the world around them

species group of animals that can have babies together

Index